My ELEPHANT LIFE

by FB Smit

illustrated by Brooke O'Neill

PICTURE WINDOW BOOKS

a capstone imprint

Published by Picture Window Books,
an imprint of Capstone
1710 Roe Crest Drive, North Mankato,
Minnesota 56003
capstonepub.com

Library of Congress Cataloging-in-Publication Data is available on the Library of Congress website.
ISBN: 9798875239410 (hardcover)
ISBN: 9798875239366 (paperback)
ISBN: 9798875239373 (ebook PDF)

Summary: Find out what it's like to be the largest mammal on land and follow an African forest elephant for a day.

Editorial Credits
Editor: Christianne Jones
Designer: Kay Fraser
Production Specialist: Whitney Schaefer

Printed and bound in China. PO 6461

Nice to meet you. I'm an African elephant. As you can see from my size, I have A LOT to show you. After all, I'm the largest mammal on land.

In water, only one animal is bigger. Any guesses what animal that is?

It's a whale! Speaking of water, I can swim. My webbed feet and powerful legs push me through the water.

Even though I'm heavy, I have natural buoyancy. I can even breathe under water. Do you know how?

I use my trunk as a snorkel!

My trunk is my upper lip and my nose.
I have an incredible sense of smell.
It's even better than a bloodhound's.

Out of the water, my trunk is my hand. I grab tree bark, grass, leaves, and flowers for a snack. I'm an herbivore. I may not eat meat, but I do eat often.

Guess how many hours I eat every day?

Eighteen! I stroll for miles with my herd seeking food and water. It takes a lot to fuel this enormous body.

If food is out of reach,
my trunk is a crane.

What do you think I do if I can't reach food I want to eat?

I put my big body to use! I weigh almost 15,000 pounds, so I bump and shake the tree until the fruit falls to the ground.

I also use another body part to help me get food. What do you think it is?

My tusks! I use them to tear bark from trees.

I also use my tusks to dig up soil. Certain soil has salt and minerals that keep me healthy.

By the way, my tusks grow and grow. Can you imagine if your teeth never stopped growing?

When you eat a lot, you poop a lot. I poop about 1 ton a week. Thankfully, my poop is very helpful to Earth. The seeds in my poop create new and different plant varieties.

Elephants help plants and animals in other ways too. We dig up dry riverbeds to make watering holes. The water in these beds help us and other wildlife survive during droughts.

In addition to droughts, dangers come from humans who want our tusks. It's a big reason we are endangered.

We are also losing space to human homes, and it's getting harder to find food and water.

And all this walking isn't easy under the hot sun! How do you think I cool off?

I flap my big ears!

These big ears give me excellent hearing too. However, I use another body part to help me hear as well.

What do you think it is?

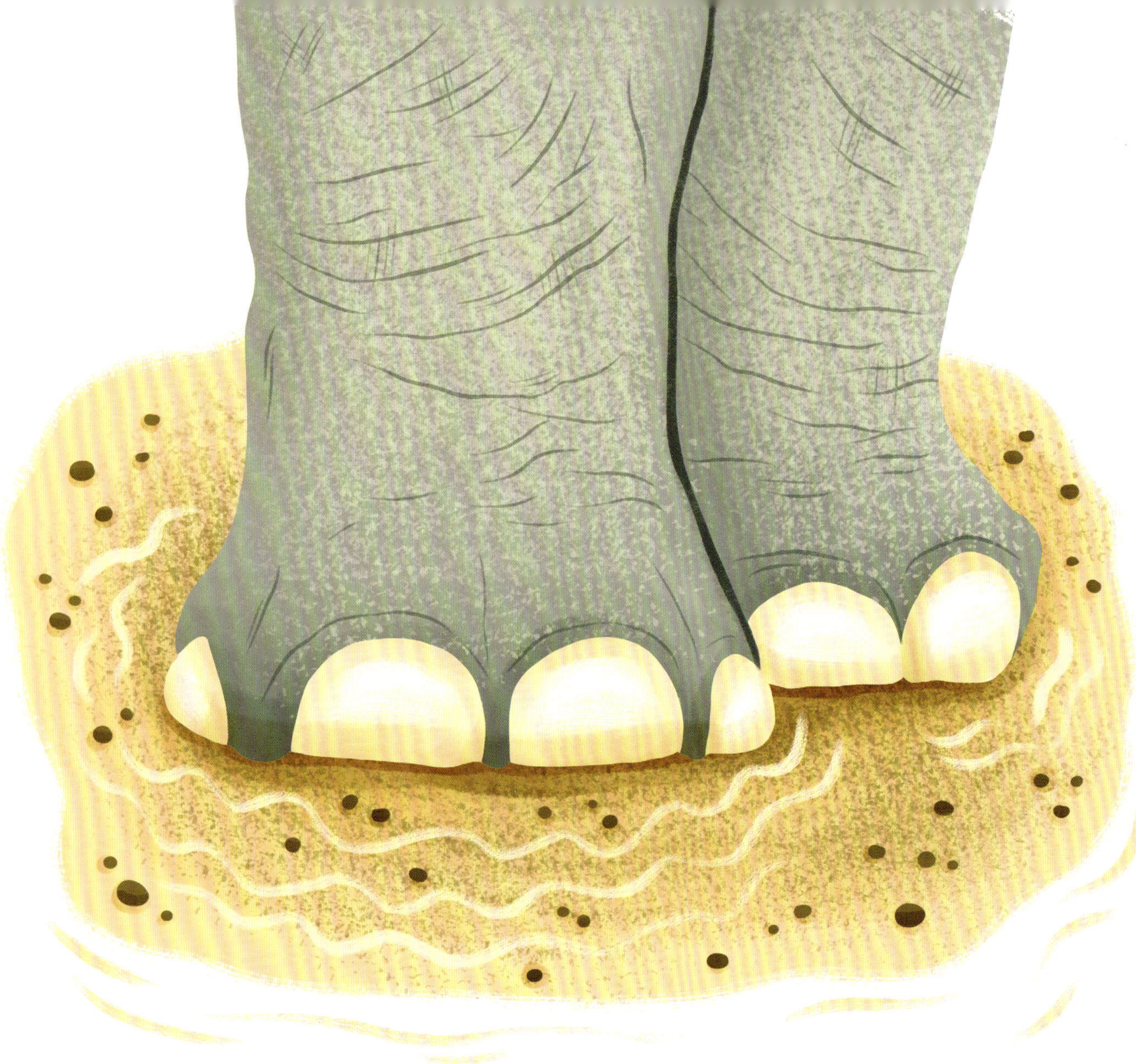

It’s my feet! They sense vibrations in the ground. I can feel the vibrations from 20 miles away or more! This signal alerts me to distant storms and dangers to keep me and my herd safe.

Wait . . . I feel something coming!

BOOM! A rainstorm!

After the storm passes, the herd drinks, plays, and cools off in the water. But I don't like to stay clean. Clean skin makes it easier for bugs to bite and the sun to burn.

Guess what I cover myself in?

Mud! The mud protects my sensitive skin.

After another water break, we'll go look for more food.

Thanks for spending the day with me!

Excellent Elephant Facts

- Elephants sleep as little as two hours a day.
- Every day, elephants eat more than 200 pounds of food and drink 30–50 gallons of water.
- Elephants communicate in lots of ways, including a trumpet call.
- There are three types of elephants. They are the African savanna (or bush) elephant, the African forest elephant, and the Asian elephant.
- Females and young elephants travel in herds. Male elephants usually travel alone.
- African elephant trunks have two "fingers" at the tip of their trunks. Asian elephant trunks have one.
- Elephant skin is very thick, and the folds and wrinkles hold water to help keep them cool.

Glossary

buoyancy (BOI-uhn-see)—the power to float

drought (DROUT)—a long period of weather with little or no rain

endangered (en-DAYN-jerd)—high risk of disappearing in the wild

herbivore (HUR-buh-vor)—an animal that eats only plants

herd (HURD)—a large group of animals that lives or moves together

mammal (MAM-uhl)—a warm-blooded animal that breathes air and produces milk for its baby

mineral (MIN-ur-uhl)—a substance found naturally in the ground

tusk (TUHSK)—a very long tooth that sticks out when the mouth is closed

vibration (vye-BRAY-shuhn)—a fast movement back and forth

About the Author

FB Smit is an author, blogger, and a preschool teacher. When she's not engaging with the littles at school, she's incubating her real and made-up stories. She's grateful for her husband and children who teach her about life and who thicken her stories' plots. At home near Atlanta, Georgia, FB does her best to avoid buying more houseplants and drinking way too much tea. Connect with her at fbsmit.com.

About the Illustrator

Brooke O'Neill is an illustrator and graphic designer who has illustrated greeting cards, stickers, and more than twenty children's books. When she's not drawing, Brooke loves spending time with her kids, husband, and pets in the suburbs of Chicago. Other interests include playing the ukulele, reading, insects, astrology, sharks, plants, and watching movies. If she wasn't an artist, she would definitely be a professional organizer!